THE
CATARACTS

Also by Raymond McDaniel

Murder (a violet)
Saltwater Empire
Special Powers and Abilities

THE
CATARACTS

Raymond McDaniel

COFFEE HOUSE PRESS
Minneapolis
2018

Coffee House Press books are available to the trade through our primary distributor, Consortium Book Sales & Distribution, cbsd.com or (800) 283-3572. For personal orders, catalogs, or other information, write to info@coffeehouse press.org.

Coffee House Press is a nonprofit literary publishing house. Support from private foundations, corporate giving programs, government programs, and generous individuals helps make the publication of our books possible. We gratefully acknowledge their support in detail in the back of this book.

LIBRARY OF CONGRESS CATALOGING-IN-PUBLICATION DATA

Names: McDaniel, Raymond, 1969– author.
Title: The cataracts / Raymond McDaniel.
Description: Minneapolis : Coffee House Press, 2018.
Identifiers: LCCN 2017030788 | ISBN 9781566894937
Classification: LCC PS3613.C3868 A6 2018 | DDC 811/.6—dc23
LC record available at https://lccn.loc.gov/2017030788

PRINTED IN THE UNITED STATES OF AMERICA

24 23 22 21 20 19 18 17   1 2 3 4 5 6 7 8

Contents

THE
CATARACTS

Projection Box

A mattress unrolled on the floor.
At the head, a window.
At the feet, a mirror.

When moonlight fills the window,
moonlight fills the mirror,
and the mirror fills the box with light.

Without color, only with shade,
what happens outside the box
doubles the box, suffuses the box.

Light is not light.
Light is only one way things radiate,
so light is an object falling apart.

The light of the moon
is the light of the sun,
which is the sun collapsing.

So the moonlight was not of the moon,
nor was the mirror of the moon,
nor the light it reflected again.

Yet in the mirror, the window.
Through the window, the moon.
Between and because: light.

Do you know where you are,
if you know that wherever you are,
you are lost?

Decimation

But it was really a lot of time in either a library or

an ocean—

sometimes I would walk out of the library and into

the ocean—they were that close.

What they had in common: more books than people,

more waves than people,

neither empty but populated thickly by things that weren't people.

And both free to the public.

In a library I learned the origin of the verb *decimate:*

to remove one-tenth of any given number,

usually soldiers set to be punished

for a group offense to preserve the republic.

A tenth of the ocean is nothing to the ocean,

though it is also the size of an ocean.

A tenth taken away doesn't seem so many,

though it must to the taken and those from whom

they are taken. Those who remain are also punished:

to remember whatever sin consigned the others

to oblivion, and the obliterated. A tenth, its remnant.

People were so rare in the library

and—if you walked far enough down

the shore—so rare on the beach, so few

relative to the ocean, infinitely divisible.

All the world felt like a remnant of a previous world.

Knowing that I was the youngest meant knowing

I would become the remnant of a previous world.

Now there are too many, though that is a problem

with no just solution it is also—

like a wave flattened under the weight of a wave

or a book that falls to dust when you open it—

a sin that will punish itself.

Overdue

the house unsound confused inside and out the old man

        & the sea with cracks wide

      enough for snakes the king james

    bible screens instead of windows or

       the magic mirror of m.c.

      escher an oak slowly growing through the roof

the almanac & a door seething with fire ants

        the red and the black matter

     you could hear shifting the naked ape

       when it rained

water would pearl on the walls of the ship of fools

    it wasn't our house it was just the house

     we lived in great expectations

Agfa Lupe 8x

I sat as close to the television as I could.
I knew of what prismatic cascade it was made.

Likewise I read by placing my face
to the book, as if in prayer.

The gift I was given looked like a shot glass
and functioned like an eyeglass.

First thought: eight by some unknown,
a mystery resolved by the optics.

Then eight times, the number
of sightings allowed before vanishment.

The loupe was made to vanish distance
but I could do that, uncorrected.

The company that manufactured it vanished,
along with the purposes of these tools

I have in a tin box, which is now vintage,
obsolescent as what it contains.

No, the box isn't obsolescent, nor
the functions for which the tools were made.

Just this box, just these tools: antique.
Everything has a number of times

it can be used for the reason it was made.
What was this little table monocle for?

To make for you a vision of what I saw
because I could not, without device, see.

Near, the puppet says, and capers away
to give a flat surface depth, and then *Far*.

Wait Until Dark

In the film adaptation of the play *Wait Until Dark*

the role of the blind protagonist is played

by the sighted Audrey Hepburn but it is that property

of her character—that Susy is a blind woman—

upon which the whole of the plot depends.

Yet this is also why any reconstruction of the plot

is meaningless. Many things occur, and each

is precipitated or enabled by the fact that Susy

cannot see, a condition with which the audience

is primed to sympathize by seeing all those things

that Susy cannot, though in fact the villains of the film

deploy all the standard mechanisms of deceit

more effectively than they capitalize on Susy's

sightlessness, so that the implication moves from

the pity engendered to how easily one can lie

to the blind to dread at the realization of how easily

anyone can lie to or about anyone else. And to this

Susy's blindness is secondary or a metaphor,

a use unpalatable to those actually blind themselves.

But the film is called *Wait Until Dark* and the dark

for which it is most famous is not the one in which

Susy lives but the one she perpetuates upon her enemies.

As she shatters the bulbs of every light in her home

the film truly begins, and those who saw the movie

in theatrical release enjoyed or flinched from the fact

that the proprietors dimmed the house lights accordingly,

until for a long moment the last antagonist and every

member of the audience waited in the condition Susy

has manufactured in the home she seeks to escape,

which is the larger home she cannot exit, which is darkness.

In the final moments of *Wait Until Dark* the ways and means

of light become vitally important: the rasp of a match

and the gasoline Susy flings not to enhance light but have it

extinguished, and at last the forgotten neglected bulb

in the refrigerator, whose door has been propped open

for just this purpose. When you are in forever dark

it can be difficult to remember or imagine how stupid

the world is with light, how gratuitous and cavalier

light is, and it is by this light that we the audience see

Susy weep as she realizes how, for all her intelligence,

she will die because she forgot about the refrigerator.

The face of Audrey Hepburn is famous and some measure

of the power of *Wait Until Dark* is the sick permission

to stare at the face of Audrey Hepburn as she suffers

one threat and indignity after another, to stare at her

naked terror and rage and triumph, as if because

she knew she could not see us she was free to express

sentiments imperfect to a face celebrated for perfection.

This effect is achieved not by blindness but by performance.

This performance is achieved by having stared at the blind,

having studied them, having looked long into faces

that did not look back so as to look as if she was not

looking back as we stared at her. Poor Susy, brave Susy.

See in the residual light all that radiates from the blind,

the unseeing face, blind only because it looks to us so.

Landlords

I choose instead *Land-Lords,* to make strange the relation between
the former and the latter, to make apparent again the yoke under which
you labor.

In his malevolent disinterest, the first Land-Lord was everywhere and
nowhere we ever needed him to be, neither in the repair of the air com-
pressor nor of the unsealable door, in the removal of neither vermin nor
lice. We curse him with sudden terror, wasting diseases, and fever to
destroy his eyes and drain his strength.

The second Land-Lord was made of equal parts benevolence and caprice,
and understood not the consequence of either. We curse him to plant
seed on his retirement farmland in vain; we enjoin his enemies to eat it,
so that he shall enjoy no fulfillment and his children wither and weep in
the dust.

The third Land-Lord was a great court of priests and courtiers, whose
ruler was fantastic and vague and moved like the mist, neither could it
be grasped or wrestled. It placed Agatha Christie novels in the laundry
room and maintained the pool area only diffidently, for it did not care
who we were, only that we were one of many. We curse it to be defeated
by its enemies, to be overcome by the clannish solidarity of Russian
immigrants, who did care who we were and who cared for us and for
whom we cared; these immigrants you hate we assign to rule over you,
and curse you to flee from them, even when they pursue you not.

The fourth Land-Lord was kind, but was in thrall to yet another Land-
Lord, and in the name of the fourth Land-Lord we curse this ruler in a
distant land seven times over, to break his stubborn pride.

The fifth Land-Lord was a jackal in human form, who held those in his
dominion as less than jackals, deserving less than the weakest and most
lame of jackals. For his indoor-outdoor carpet and his E. L. Mustee
Durastall we make the sky above him like iron and the ground beneath
him like bronze and curse his strength to be spent in vain.

The sixth Land-Lord was as the fifth, but even more vile and unholy, with his cinderblock walls and his dwelling lodged halfway into the dust of the earth, and so we multiply his afflictions, as his sins deserve.

The seventh Land-Lord was a man of God, merciful and humble, and we bless him and his earthly works.

The eighth Land-Lord spoke as a man of God but grew bitter malice in his heart like a weed, and piled increase upon increase, for his lust was for rent and not to be like the Lord. We send wild animals against him, who shall rob him of his children and destroy his cattle, or whatever.

The ninth Land-Lord was of a people who knew not God, and whose ways were monstrous, for they would bathe their children in the heat of the summer and leave the filthy water standing for a month while they pilgrimaged to Wisconsin to worship their strange gods. In this and in many other ways they broke their covenant with us, so we send a plague among them, and consign them to the hands of those who would spill their blood and see them destroyed from the earth.

The tenth Land-Lord was a spirit who rejected the Lord, and was filled with poison and malice, and who squatted like a low beast beneath the decaying cell in which he imprisoned us, and sent up foul gasses to poison us, and when we fled weeping would feign to weep with us, but his tears were false and the color of blood. He is a thing detestable, and we curse him struck dead.

Then all the people shall say *Amen.*

Blind Man's Bluff

The legend among the sisters goes like this:

That the younger one did not *mean*
to walk the elder off the seawall
but did.

That it was an accident. But

it would have been an odd sort of accident,
since the younger child had her eyes wide open
and the older child, my mother,
had hers closed tight.

Nothing my mother did could have been an accident,
because she only did what she was told to do,
and nothing her sister did could have been an accident,
since she was doing the telling.

Bear in mind this was my mother's telling,
to make us laugh and distract us
as we too walked or were walked into air.

You know the game, you've likely played it,
it is a killer of time and cheap.

You know what exculpatory lies you would tell—

I told her to stop,
I didn't know she was so close to the edge.

Tears and protests.

But either she was paying attention
and it was malice
or she was not paying attention
and it was depraved indifference.

When my mother walked off the edge of the wall

it might as well have been the edge of the world

even though at the beach you are always aware of the edge
because you can always hear it:
the sea the stupid wall exists to stop.

Still, hearing it would not stop your body
from falling or help you know
whether you were falling a few feet or ten feet or
from the surface of the earth itself.

When I asked her if it hurt,
she always said the fear was worse than the pain,
laughed it off by saying

I just had the breath knocked out of me.

If you don't know that it's about to happen
or that such a thing can happen at all,
to be breathless is terror:

you are trying to do something you have never had to try to do
and you cannot do it
and everything you want to do
—scream, cry, call for help—
you cannot.

When we asked to be told this story over and over again
my father would attempt to empathize
by reminding us that when he was a child
he built a pair of artificial wings
and leapt from the roof of his house and so
he too had the breath knocked out of him.

And my mother would make a sound
that was laughing and crying
and neither and both and say

You jumped but I was pushed.

I remember that sound, the expression
of too many things at once,
what pressure ejects from the vessel
lest the vessel explode.

It was a story we told because it was funny
and it was good to laugh because laughter
kept the vessel from exploding.

But then her sister would say
I didn't push you,
you walked off the wall by yourself.

No one wants to hear of one's suffering
that you did it to yourself.
Even when it is true, it is a lie.

When you call it "blindman's bluff"
it could be that you are speaking of the trick or the cliff,
the bluff I bluffed you off of.

But the name of the game is "blindman's buff,"
and *buff* means to *push,*

a phrase deteriorated over time,
each retelling changing the meaning of the game
without changing its rules.

That undifferentiated exhalation
is what saves the lungs from explosion,
an expression that is one thing and the other,

what she could not for long moments say
because of what she did not see,
falling whether she jumped or was pushed,
saving herself by being breathless,

because then it did not, would not matter
whether she had wanted to laugh or to cry.

Haven

Is the name for the place of safety or refuge.

Though refuge from what is unclear, unspecified,

it matters in that the nature of a haven depends

on what you are fleeing from but it doesn't matter

in that once there, whatever you flee cannot—

what?

That might matter: whether whatever I was fleeing

could not get to me because I was in haven

or could not see me because I was in haven

or maybe it was that once I was in haven I didn't exist.

This haven was a part of the woods where the trees

were younger and so we called it *haven,* as if

the older trees had preserved this place just

for the younger trees. Even though we knew

it didn't work like that, it looked as if it should,

and in this even though it was forested the haven

resembled the haven from which the word comes,

the haven that is a water-word. A haven is a port

or a harbor, water shallower and safer than open

ocean, a crèche for wavelets, a bay for babies.

Haven is where we went for sticks we enhanced

by calling them staves, the word for wood

from which one makes a bow, but made of

as little wood as possible. Haven was sacred,

so we could take a little timber but not too much,

and of that wood make a shaping. For a bow

you need a dense wood and you need to know

that wood well: if it fails it will explode, which

sounds fantastic, excessive, but if there is a knot

or a warp or something unseen in the weave

of the wood when you pull it back it will not

just break or splinter, it will shatter.

You want all that force and more, but you want it

stable, transferable. A carpenter's children

let loose in the woods are dangerous,

for they have words for everything they love,

and the word for one who works wood in this way

is bowyer, and a bow carved from a single stave

can look to the unfamiliar like anything but what it is

until you string it. Once strung everyone knows

the smiling shape and the function, the suborned stick.

Not everything that can be a weapon is only a weapon,

nor any word the wood with which it shares the world.

I never shot at a living creature and never would.

A nocked arrow was a portal to haven: the arms opened

to the anchor point, a posture in which I could stand

forever, waiting. It is as if that in-drawn breath,

unlike all others, would never require an exhalation.

The limb draws the line, the arm points to a point,

space is drawn by releasing the hold on the drawn shape.

Who would teach archery to a half-blind boy?

As the ability to discern detail fades,

the eye's emphasis on motion increases.

To stand at anchor point is to be a stilled ship

in a haven, to see is to forget the miracle by which

moving things always seem to be in motion

and stationary things always seem stationary.

There are increasingly complex machines for this

archaic task—wheels and pulleys, pins and mirrors,

a bow of parts and pieces, not one stave shaped

like a stick until strung. But if you rest in that recurve,

wait in haven, wait for water, wait for wind,

if you wait until something in the great green and blue

blur moves. The limb will draw the line. The line

will collapse the space. *There* will become *here*.

Of course I confused it with heaven.

The Interchangeable World of the Micronauts

What half-blind is like:

like two microscopes in my head

each with differently stuck objectives.

They enable the small and the very small

and reduce everything else to blur and shade.

Yet you can train even this.

Train it to spot the shape of sharks' teeth,

of which there are many samples and many shapes

but not as many as flecks of sand, pieces of shell.

I have hundreds plucked from the shore.

But in the same beach I buried a toy

and never found it again. A tiny toy:

articulate, a translucent man, a smallness

to whom the world was an unbounded wonder.

Blemished and damaged I would hold him up

and say *He is broken* and anyone who could see

would say *He looks fine to me.*

But they can see well, not finely.

Look at his face, etched and serrated

by that gargantuan saw.

The cracked shell of his translucent skin

buried in rubble now, and those teeth,

all that remain of terrible and invisible jaws.

Psychotic Mood Swing

Shout down the valley.
Crowd out the mountain.
Array and display the glade.

I heard, I heard, I heard.
Tony Tony jump around.
Help me find what can't be found.

Viridescent

Of the emerald blur I could distinguish no sense

save names and purposes, plant lore.

Wolf's foot, stag's horn, running pine,

whose spores are flash-explosive.

Fiddleheads, ash for forest glass.

Resurrection fern, one hundred years without water.

Sand cedar, from which bows could be bent.

Live oak, curved for shipbuilding.

Black mangrove, black in its salt-extruding heart.

White ash, from which one could cut a staff or a bat.

Rum cherry, cabinets of which intoxicated their contents.

False box, the butcher's block.

Devil stick, of universal use, the angelica tree.

Witch hazel, diviner of water.

Black nightshade, killer of children.

Even the leaves of bastard indigo and wood violet: green.

Like grass or emeralds, viridescent.

Artichoke, asparagus, avocado.

Dark green is dark green.

Hooker's green, laurel green.

Light green is light green.

Myrtle, mint, pine.

(Not teal, nothing is teal.)

Olive.

Celadon, hunter, copper.

Verdigris. The emerald blur.

Because it was green it was grass

and because it was grass it grew.

Destiny and Mystique

The question I would not answer:

    Are you a boy or

        a girl are you a boy or a girl

and my interrogator would hit me in the face

    alternating fists with each cycle of questioning

      and might have done so

    even had I answered

but I didn't like the question and so

      Fuck him

    or at least that's what I said

        to myself

  as I crushed ice and put it in a bag

to place over the periorbital hematoma

      of my left eye

because even though he had been switching hands

    apparently could only aim with one

      are you a lefty or a righty

        a lefty or a righty I sang

  as I read one-eyed

about how the Brotherhood of Evil Mutants

planned on getting this party

(by which I and they meant a better and more just world)

started

by killing some pompous senator

and whether it would or wouldn't happen

all came down to the actions

of an elderly blind precognitive mutant

whose lover and best friend

was a queer blue shape-shifting terrorist

it was 1981

and all this for fifty cents

Destiny wore a gold mask & could see the future

and as my eye swelled shut

I wondered what the future would look like

when you couldn't see

and I wondered about Mystique

and what it meant to never have to change shape

for the person you loved

because the person you loved couldn't see you

anyway and didn't care

so when my mother asked me what happened

I said

Well Kitty Pryde has come back from the future

to change the past

and she said

No what happened to your eye

and I said

Well the Brotherhood is fighting for mutant liberation

and she said

OK are they good guys or bad guys

are they good or are they bad

are they guys or are they good

are they bad or are they brothers

are they X-Men or are they bad guys

and I said

they are mutants

they are all X-Men to me

Vertumnal

Vertumnus, god of gardens, a whom out of a what.
From dirt I declare I can make anything:
the quartz and loam and severed insects,
the gourds and grasses, up from dirt
the hares and the dogs and the men
who can run down neither hares nor dogs
yet somehow manage to kill and eat both.
Of dirt, all these. In quadrants, exhibited,
I declare all outdoors my garden.
Glass it in, I threaten, but with water and light
my garden will grow and die and grow by dying
and thus subsist forever and ever.
In the garden stands the thing that stands for human,
to scare away hares and dogs, to be the garden's god.
Only a man would look for a god in grass and see a man.
The dog runs for the hare and the rabbit runs from the dog,
one for its dinner and the other for its life.
But a man just stands and attributes himself to god.
The search for Vertumnus reveals the rendering,
then the god rendered, and only then the renderer.

Space

Stand in the doorway of the Santa Maria del Fiore

on a beautiful day.

Stupid perfect clouds in a stupid perfect sky.

Gaze straight ahead.

The boy had rendered on a square wooden panel

the baptistery of San Giovanni

and in the center of this panel drilled one small hole.

His friends he had directed: with one hand hold the panel

to your eye, so that the rendered building faces

the actual building, and with the other hand hold

a mirror.

The panel with the left hand, the mirror with the right.

Peer through the hole in the panel and see

the baptistery of San Giovanni!

Slowly bring the mirror into your line of sight

and see again the baptistery of San Giovanni!

The place and the reflection of the painting of the place.

The same, the same.

Even the clouds move across the polished surface

of the painted sky.

I will show you where it is because of where it must be

Of objects in space, consider the rate of their motion. Because I could not keep my eye on the ball, because I could not see the ball until it struck me, but could keep my eye on the ball metaphorically—could focus and attend. Because I could climb but could not see the ground beneath me and would rather sit in the limbs of a tree or at the top of a slide than venture down, since I could not see how far I might have to fall. Because my handwriting was imperceptible without magnification, but, magnified, proved impeccable. Because I could not magnify everything by standing right next to it, I knew leaves but not proverbial trees, knew vague light but not the actual moon. In space I was at a loss but saw in space other spaces. How, I asked, am I supposed to know what things are if I can't know where they are? He sat me down at the table where we liked to draw. He showed me a drawing of a place called Castrovalva, but I only heard castle-valve, and thought of village as a machine, and when he said look at this and tell me what is strange about it, I stared and stared but didn't see anything strange. I stared until I moved into the village I saw, I saw through its walls, I turned the drawing upside down and saw a mountain crush the village into the lake of the sky, I saw the villagers come and go. One day I saw that there was no difference between distant and close in the castle-valve, that difference the undrawn world must inevitably possess, and I didn't understand how that drawing was possible. Is this what is strange? I asked.

He read, "This is Castrovalva from without, but even more so it is Castrovalva from within."

He said, *I will show you where it is because of where it must be.*

Castle-Valve

the city of castle-valve sits or grips the mountain's edge
so that its walls orange and ochre both
hold down the mountain & structure the sky
anvil-upended clouds & the four-cornered towers of castle-valve
capture their rains
the clouds billow and dissolve as they race
overhead & underneath
the city that hinges the mountain shut
door that opens to the sky
that pours and constricts water from rain to lake
city of hundreds doubled city of thousands
castle-valve cloistered
four corners four windows
inside & out
above & below
a door with two sides and no exits

you cannot exit the castle-valve by means of entrances
beneath the city of castle-valve lies Castrovalva
tunnels and sinks
one's city is one's home
the home of one's home is also one's home
the valve of the castle opens upon the castle

the script of the city finds us outside its walls
and requires we fall through falling
though falling of the slowest most masterful sort
wind-bent branches of the gorge
gross of grapes & pine
loose stones fill the valley carved by larger looser stone
run down the mountain to the crevasse
from altitude almost airless to moss & pine & peat
damp the holes in the stone made by fern & branch
the atrium's arteries full of the water fallen
from the heights upon the heights of castle-valve

& sprung from the rocks beneath it
if you turn in the air as you fall you will see the clouds
gather over the belittling city and the tinsmithing women
who fling water over the wall
its drops & rivulets racing toward you
as you race away & break or breach the surface of the sink
the sun shudders in the dim disk of the sky
the ring of rock at which center sits the city of castle-valve
reflected and broken on the skin of the sink
reassembled as you descend

the tunnels and caves of castle-valve
flooded with water
when you emerge you have entered the city of Castrovalva
when you submerge you have entered the city of Castrovalva
you cannot get out in that once out you cannot think
your way back in

above as below
doubled
sororal

you see yourself seeing
one sister sees in her sister a seeing
and says as they fall *welcome*
if this city is not my city
if my sister is not my sister
if her city is not my city
where then shall I go to make a home

Makers

ghel:

To shine, with derivates referring to colors, bright materials, gold, and
bile or gall.

Gleam. Glimpse. Glint. Glimmer. Glitter. Glisten. Glister. Glass. Glaze.
Gloss. Glance. Glad. Glee. Glow. Glower. Gloat. Gloaming. Glide.
Glissade. Glib.

Working a forge for gold, working a fire, a blacksmith or glazier will cover
an eye.

A cyclops cannot tell the difference between a painting of the world and
the world.

A glassblower risks cataracts.

The problem with cataracts is glare.

Cataracts

When I asked him why he had to go
to the hospital, he gave me a new word

cataracts

and I turned the word clicking under my tongue
like a lock's tumbler

it fell fast like its other meaning

and rather than explain cataracts with words
he cut out a pair of lenses from some draftsman's opaque sheet
and taped them to my glasses

Is that what you see I asked, barely able to see now at all

and afterwards I wasn't afraid of what would happen to him
in the hospital but of driving walking being tempted
to look at the sun made dull and frosted and clouded

I was sure that even with cataracts the sun would kill him

but when he went to the hospital to receive new eyes
by having an aspect of his eyes cut away

instead he was told that the film of his lungs
was as milky as his eyes, which though white
on the sheet as shiny as the draftsman's film

meant bad

was like bad fruit, spotted and black

and so they put him on his stomach and cut him open
and broke and cut out his ribs and left something better

because it was emptier.

* * *

Hospitals are for the sick but also where the sick get sick
and he was so wounded and so tired
he became sick with unwelcome life

every time he came home he went away again
because new things required breaking and he kept getting sick

so while he was away I learned to wake up very early
and to boil water on the stove and to make tea
alternately lemon or mint though too sweet in either case

and sit in his chair and wait

and I learned to practice feeling his death.

"Nearly dead" is an impossible condition as I realized
even then

because he would be dead or he would not be dead
but we were told many times that he was going to die.

A year later when he came home and when we knew he would stay
he had acquired the habits
of soap operas and antibiotic soap
with which we all had to wash our hands incessantly

and with warm water and antibiotic soap
we filled the cavity of his chest and gently agitated him
and then drained the solution through the hole

they had left in his back for just this purpose.

* * *

Other things changed as well

for when you are broken and know you have been broken
the act of breaking can make you kind or cruel
and while he was made kind

because we were all broken by the cost of his having been broken
as a group we became suspicious of the unbroken

while another year passed
while all he could do was ask me what I was reading
what I had seen

and after a year he said he was going to the hospital again

and when I asked him why he said

cataracts

though he had in the hospital been broken
and wounded and made sick enough to die
many, many times

and though as a result of having been broken and wounded and sick
for a year

his hands with which he drew were for the act of drawing destroyed
curled into claws barely able to grasp a pencil

and the job for which he would have been required to draw
was gone
and the reasons for which he needed to see
no longer mattered

broken diminished exhausted unable to work

he still wanted to see

and so went back and was cut once again.

* * *

I remember he was delighted and astonished
to have the detail of the world restored

the brightness and the light simple lucid radiant

and he lived for years and grew tired of much

but never of sight.

* * *

After he died I dreamed of him twice

and in the first dream he had acquired the power of flight
and flew with the same delight with which he saw
but in the second dream he was sitting
in the very chair I sat in the year he kept dying

and coming back to life

so I bent down to look up at him and the irises
of his eyes were the white of unsplit light

and then they faded like coils of cut filament
giving up their heat
and it is the heat that makes the light
save for when the light is expended

when I was small and wanted to look at the sun
he said if you want to stare at the sun

and not go blind you look not at its light

but what it illuminates the world the moon

never the thing itself and always its reflection.

Unfurl

Your souls, if you have them,
depart without having spoken.
They issue reels and loops
of thread, filaments lengthened
by longing, coming apart
in the sky like the tails of a shower.

When it speaks, a soul sounds
like this looks: a boule of copper—hot,
falling to ribbons, the core
drawn finer and finer, until
you can see its tongues, hissing.

Fortifications of the Land of Grasses and Flowers

It seems like summer will kill the city,
that this city will be the last city,
whatever left standing a radiation shade
of something unutterably prior.

Sunset behind the last city
is fourteen thousand fingers of shadow
creeping across the river
and attenuated rivulets of light.

Sunset behind the last city
sets the westward walls on fire
or the illusion of fire trapped
in the glass.

Sunset commences and no one
steps outside to welcome it
for no one welcomes it,
not even orphans or urchins.

These, who have toiled and scurried
in its glare, know that even
its absence will leave the stone and steel
boiling, the oranges scalding in their skin.

Drawn thin as a needle the sunlight
punctures, the buildings shimmer and bake.
The people who leave them will stumble,
like children disgorged from an oven.

Replica of Vintage Sleeper Car

I prefer the company of someone who says *I am sane, but the world is insane* to the company of someone who says *I am moral, but the world is immoral.* This is not because I believe the world is insane but not immoral. It is because in narrating how the world is insane, the person who believes in her sanity will admit how that sanity is compromised by the insane world, whereas in narrating how the world is immoral, the person who believes in his morality can grow even more convinced of it, the more he details the moral failings of the world he occupies.

The time and expense that this reconstruction required: immense, and effectual. But the motion is approximate at best, and what passes for the sky fails to be the sky almost perfectly.

Look Up

For a model of a gravity well, picture an actual well.

That the moon is minor, that the moon is lesser:

do not pity the motherfucking moon because it orbits you.

From the bottom of a well, whatever sun you can see

looks like the moon. Most of the plane of the sky?

Tiled with darkness. What interrupts the moon?

The face of whoever threw you down this well.

You cannot have a fair fight from the bottom of a well.

Whoever sits at the well's lip can tip pebbles upon you.

Gravity does the rest. You can collect the pebbles, yes.

You can throw them out of the well lest you drown in pebbles.

But try to throw a rock from the bottom of a well.

Gravity does the rest. The moon is sick to death:

the object of the moon is tired of being objectified.

Look, you are bigger than the moon. It's measurable.

But you are not so big you cannot fit down a well.

The moon goes away and the moon comes back.

That great floating weight in the sky? It is the sky.

It costs the sky nothing to fall down upon you.

The Commons

The revenge I wanted to take was not an eye for an eye

but for an eye, a mind.

The opposite of property is theft, but so is property.

Property requires the occupation of space by matter.

I regret all the property I trespassed

and having curtsied ask for an apology from the law and an apologia for it.

Trespass to person, no, or only incidentally.

Trespass to chattel when I am the chattel myself, no,

for working in the place gives possession of the place, or should.

Trespass to land and the chattel of the building that stands upon it.

There was nothing in anyone's house I wanted to steal,

no sleeping body I wanted to see,

for it is perverse to want such things and of all

with such wants are none who should have them met.

This property was public

and I thought it was dumb luck that I was never caught or killed

in the act of walking in and out and over and under and around.

It was not luck but status and it was dumb to ever believe otherwise.

But it is an old right, to wander, and should be everyone's.

In compensation for abiding the rules of this building from the hours of
    8 until 5

we should claim it with the sunset.

The cooling tar on the roof,

the infolding plants of the botanical gardens,

the whir of the machine that cleans the pool,

and the time stolen to keep it all standing.

Fontanel

In the first story
I am in a terrifying fight
but when you talk
about being in a fight
people want to know
what the fight was about
or be stupidly reassured
that the other person started it
but it never really matters
or it matters before
the fight or after the fight
but it says nothing
about the fight itself
which is always two animals
trying to hurt without being hurt.

If you can say you won
even though you recall weeping
and heaving for breath
certain you could no longer breathe
but had the strange presence of mind
to be grateful
that the sand of the beach
was not so hard-packed
that you had to worry
about cracking open the head
of the boy you were fighting
because you didn't want to kill him
though everything you did
proved otherwise
and yet you worried about the softness
of the sand
and whether you would twist
your ankle which you thought
would be painful even though

you were already cut and concussed and
bleeding freely from your mouth
and exhausted and absently
cataloging which parts
of you would work and
for how much longer
how much longer
because you needed to keep
the boy's head in the crook of your elbow
until he went to sleep
and you were already so tired
and you even rested your head
against the sand
and held the boy's head
to your chest with one arm
while fending off with the other
his desperate grip
waiting to see which of you would sleep
first and for how long
if you can say
that is winning then I won.

I thought This is like rescuing
a drowning man
because the ocean
was right there and I had been trained
to do that to rescue swimmers
from the sea even though
I was drowning a boy
on dry land.

The other story is about a little girl
just ten months old
who had been left in my care
and with whom I had lived
since the first week of her life
and though she knew me

as well as she knew her mother
or her father
she had never before been
without both at once
had never been alone with me
or maybe ever even alone
with only one other person
but her mother and her father
had somewhere they needed to be
and so for a while
I would be her custodian
or guardian or companion
and while I knew what she liked to do
with her newfound ability to stand
was to listen to funk
or anything with a conspicuous beat
and dance
I did not know how long that joy
would work
and you cannot know
as a child dances uncertainly
but bravely enough
for the first few minutes after
her mother and father have left her
how long her courage
will last or how she perceives time
or absence or if you
are doing the right thing
to encourage her to keep dancing
or to pick her up and dance
with her into and out of the rooms
where she wanted to go
and in which she did not find
her mother or father.

There is no sound like a crying human baby
and if you believe there is

you are not a human.
Responding to that cry
as if there is nothing else like it
is how you know what animal
you are and you are the animal
responsible for this animal
who seems to want to die
who seems as if she cannot have
the world she wants will asphyxiate
herself or will empty
her lungs of the air
she needs to scream beyond her ability
to scream or breathe again and
if you do not know any human babies
it can sound peaceful
to hear that she cried herself
to sleep empurpled exhausted
but it was like watching her die
each breath shuddering
with the residual effort to scream
impossibly hot and coated in sweat
she fell asleep against my chest
and I knew
no human who can remember
can ever remember what the ache
she is feeling feels like
but I remembered
that boy I had choked unconscious
and that the closer to death you get
the more like an infant you become
as you panic and weep
and I thought God there are
so many things that can go wrong
but then No there are so many ways
to make things go wrong
and so much wrong I had done
or could do

but I also thought about how I held
the back of his head
and laid him on the sand
gently without thought
exactly as I held that baby's head
as I set her down to sleep
because that is how a human body
knows to hold another human body
the boy who for a while
I had killed and the little girl
who for a while
I kept alive.

Pilgrims

The poem about impermanence,
written by the itinerant poet,
comes to me translated,
as a quote in a book
in which the poet himself is itinerant,
though he resides permanently
in many equivalent quotes
in many equivalent books
that, after being shipped across oceans,
sit on shelves that have been shipped
across oceans, so that I may ponder
impermanence and be grateful
for his poor sleep, his three nights
in the stable, his meditative report:
lice, cold, horses emptying their bladders
by the head of a man whose discomfort
means no element of what he hoped
it would mean, because someone knows of it,
still.

Mine

The draglines abrade Arcadia's face.

If a mine is a mouth, the perimeter of its pit is the open jaws, the biting,
  bitter portal.

When I say *mine* I mean this, not what belongs to me, because
  this hateful hole cannot belong to anyone.

Picture the skin of a face pulled taut by gravity—the head flung back
  on its neck, the mouth flung open.

Pinned to that skin, the angles and wires and shovels, the tools.

From some mines it can take an hour or more to emerge, but an hour
  within the throat of Arcadia might as well be the ocean.

A head pulled back, water poured down the mouth until a lake laps
  at the mountains of the jaw, the mountain's carbonate ring.

Eventually the lake is a clay.

In the body of the screaming man is the poisonous matter of men.

Drowned upon descent in grit and silt and in mortal work.

Because we thought this barely-earth was ours, it went to water and it ate
  us, and when it ate us we screamed, as if surprised.

Tertullian

Surely, says Tertullian, surely:

There are more of us now than then, which is true now
   and was true then, and there are fewer inaccessible places
now than then, which makes me laugh even though I agree,
   there are now farms where once were wastes,
and I marvel at his ability to distinguish them,
   what now are fields were once forests and again, wow,
that he can tell the difference between the two,
   deserts are sewn, marshes are drained, and here I savor leaping deserts
and marshes that bite back, just you wait, Tertullian,
   single houses multiply into cities and cities
will multiply infinitely until they are earth itself,
   everywhere houses and people and government;
everywhere is civilization; and at this I wonder what
   he thinks he means.
Yet our numbers are burdensome to the world, true,
   and burdensome to us because, as he says,
everywhere we want more and more desperately,
   we suffer more and are louder in our suffering;
disease and starvation and war and earthquakes;
   these disasters are the remedy for the human race;
it is hard to resist their wretched, wrecked glamour,
   but surely even then these remedies were never applied equally
or fairly, but he guesses and doesn't know whether it is
   all to determine whether the nature of life is as of fire
that is more easily extinguished than rekindled;
   to determine if the living proceed from the dead
as it is clear that the dead are drawn from the living,
   and I shrug and say Well, he isn't wrong.
But Tertullian insists God is everywhere,
   and the goodness of God everywhere;
demons are everywhere, and the cursing of demons
   is everywhere; the invocation of divine judgment
is everywhere; death is everywhere and the sense of death

is everywhere; and all the world over is found
the testimony of the soul, and now I wonder
    if he knows that God and demons are like his fields and forests,
in that what looks like the latter can simply be a cultivar of the former,
    whether death is everywhere because of the life he insists
is everywhere and *awfully,*
    but this same Tertullian who accuses Herophilos of Alexandria,
the anatomist and founder of that city's medical school
    who in dissecting the human eye found several of its parts
(the cornea the retina the iris the choroid the optic nerve)
    and even speculated the *calamus scriptorius*
(so called because it resembled an instrument of writing,
    the reedlike hollow in the cranial bowl in which rested the soul,
which suggests that the body is the pen and the soul is the ink)
    of vivisecting 600 prisoners—and look, I doubt it.
If ever there were persons who came to no conclusions
    or who made no assertions we have no record of them,
perhaps these persons would be like ink without a nib
    and dissolve or disperse themselves
as an undifferentiated stain of souls
    but of those from whom we have a record or a legend
we know that sometimes they are in error
    and sometimes they simply lie. People lie, Tertullian,
and sometimes they are wrong because they lie.
    One way to be in error is to assume that what there is to know
requires that one merely look around,
    so that what one concludes is sure, because
that is what one sees, anyone could see it.
    Another way to be in error is to distrust the act of seeing
until one knows its mechanism and assume that knowing
    the mechanism is knowing whatever is seen thereby.
This is why the idea of the soul persists, Tertullian!
    You know, the soul? which is never seen?
which is everywhere! and the report of which is everywhere!
    but which cannot be to be seen.

There is but one truly serious philosophical problem

a *note?*

I won't

even leave

a *body*

Of Grasses and Flowers

The mountains of Florida were planted according to the design
whereby Floridians ponder elsewhere. In Florida
those who go back ten generations imagine
elsewhere requires mountains and plains and great cascades of ice,
and have forgotten that the ground here
can bear the weight of none of these,
and thus have one ocean that serves
as all three: heavy as the mountains,
wide as the plains, and even ice
just not right now.

Under the sea stand mountains. Over the sea, a plain.
In between, the much-changed bones of sailors
who would not learn to swim.
It will all boil and turn gelid before it freezes again.
In the future architectures of ice, the ships
will wait to thaw
and smell of weeds.

Today the cities are named after saints and succulents
and words for paradise. The citizens
are poisonous and everywhere.
Outside they would come to smell like sweat
but they are all indoors. The most Floridian
of them all even go indoors when they want
the sun.

Beneath the weight of the roads and the buildings
the not-stone of Florida slowly seethes.
Air hisses in pockets. The not-stone exhales
and on the in-breath consumes a street,
part of a stable of chariots, a plaza,
and a palazzo.

The parasitic saints and dwellers in paradise
are unaccountably, grimly enthusiastic.
Under thick slabs of safety glass
they exchange coin for potions and unguents
that promise hours of industry. They wait.

The mountain of Eden hovers six inches
above the skin of Florida, untouchable.
When it sinks, into the chasm made by its weight
will rush the astringent plains of the sea.

Descender

From five thousand feet, the island:
a model city, rivulets of steel, it aspires.

The model of the city is not a surface
on which you would want to fall.

But if you fall far enough you fall between:
rivulets into rivers, spires into stones.

At this scale you do not even know
that the island is an island. It is land.

Solid as rock though porous, riven
with tunnels, each hole atrial.

A mile beneath the city is no longer
the city's henge, but the city's chamber.

From here the city's a single stone,
its room hidden as a pock in marble.

In the room off the alley under the island
in the river: a bed and a dresser, a mirror.

A nightstand and papers, a paperweight
heavy enough to satisfy the hand.

Its shape a broken cube, steeplejacked.
Serrated to spikes and steel. This city.

Five Million Years to Earth

Also known as *Quatermass and the Pit*,

Five Million Years to Earth is a story told twice

and each telling in the middle of a longer tale,

that of Professor Barnard Quatermass, a type

anyone would recognize as an Explainer,

one of those who, in the presence of the abnormal, remains

reassuringly lucid and in the absence of the abnormal,

comes to appear strange himself. He makes old

things new and things thought new, ancient.

By the time of the events of *Five Million Years to Earth*,

Quatermass has already established his utility

in a world stranger than a postwar England wants

to acknowledge, and so when workmen excavating London

find what appear to be a paleolithic skull and a bomb

and what are in fact the fossilized remnants

of a mutated prehuman and a rocket ship,

it is Quatermass who puzzles out from the initial mystery

a greater mystery. A skull and a bomb are strange

and a mutated human and a rocket ship

are stranger still, but when you dig a pit you are obliged

to whatever you find in it, for at every layer of the pit

is proof that it was once not a hole in the ground

but the ground itself. A hole in the ground is the eye

through which the past sees the present and the present

can fall into the past, as if via an act of memory, whereby

we make sense of the insensible, looking into shadows

to explain a fear of darkness. London's riots were white fear

of brown faces, but in *Five Million Years to Earth* the alien races

are actually alien, are actually races, and for humans

the fear of the devil is the memory of the shape of the mind

of a dead race moving human bodies to forms fit to house

the mind of that murderous race long after it had torn itself

apart in hatred and lust and war. This is an altogether roundabout

explanation of more common hatreds, but to justify Quatermass

the Explainer requires a mystery, the solution to which you can intuit.

Or whose origins you can see by looking out the window.

Some mysteries require an optic-encephalogram, a device that records

and broadcasts trace impressions from the brain

of upon whomever it is placed, which is how Quatermass

learns that some fraction of living Londoners contain

trace remnants of the mutant genes of long-dead aliens

and carry also the potential to enact a telepathic mass murder

against those Londoners who do not. Well, that's one answer.

If in the present you see what you cannot believe,

you call what you see a vision, as if the means by which you would see

what cannot be there becomes synonymous with the thing

you cannot see. Pictures in the mind of one woman,

visions in the mind of the masses, a purge enabled

by a shared sense of seeing what should not be.

In *Five Million Years to Earth* Quatermass

and his allies save London and the human race

with an applied folktale, that an apparition abhors iron,

which is like saying a hard fact is the natural enemy of a vague idea.

Still, what a relief to have an explanation that is also an answer.

Ghost, ghast, demon, devil, plague, pestilence, threat, hate,

a version, a vision, a Martian, a memory, a mnemonic.

It's a mess and a mystery, we shrug, but it all ends

when a man throws a chain down a well, and we all know

that a loose chain is better than one that binds you,

that all's well that ends well, yes? No matter how it begins.

Here Comes the Flood

In *Here Comes the Flood* the painter makes the perfect village by making the perfect villagers, who know that in order to make the lake which, when still, will both reflect the village and be the surface on which the village sits, each must take up the same task, hoist to their shoulders the same tesserae, the same flat squares of sky. They look like sky because they reflect the sky, but they are lake, because they cannot stand on sky. From where you sit in the unfinished village, you cannot see the faces of the villagers who hold the lake aloft. But if the village is unfinished, how can you be sitting, where do you sit? Clearly this is not the first flood, nor the first village. Clearly, this is not the first you.

The Uncertain Value of Human Life

Behind the frozen falls:
green light through green ice.

Nothing made here,
nowhere to sleep.

Just the pale white light
ice-diffuse, indifferent.

And in the branching caves of karst:
blue light through blue water.

Transparent liquid settled flat
over heavy, blurry brine.

It looks like two rooms.
But in neither can you breathe.

Generation Mechanism

It is tedious only if you know it isn't true.

A dream is a sort of tool or device, but

every time I have this dream

there is a moment when I think the thing of which I have dreamed

and am currently dreaming is finally true—

but then in the dream I recall all the other times

I have had this dream,

including the time

when the problem posed by tidal waves

was solved simply by scale and flight,

buildings that became colossal, gargantuan,

the principle of a sea wall magnified ten thousand times.

The ten thousands, the hours and amounts.

A wave-caller who crawls across

the massive face of the architecture—

he seems real.

And by the time I remember that he cannot be real:

here comes the whole ocean.

Harbor wave, first memory, is not a wave.

It is a tide.

Before it can return, it must go away.

Drawback, its generation mechanism,

whereby amplitude = height

and the height is the weight of breaking water,

of broken water.

Even the dream of the wave is a dream of light,

of the buildings and statutes that aren't,

the legs of the colossi barrier islands,

the glassless windows of the rooms of their eyes.

The caller stands on the cliffs and shouts, *wave, wave*—

caught in the fluttering eye of the abyssal.

Like everyone, I could dream before I could see,

and now the dream and the sight are the same.

Wave after wave, zealous seams.

Downrushing, descent of water,

and the people in the village by the sea flee

as they have dreamed of fleeing, have fled before.

The descendants of the descent of water sound

like water as it flees and returns.

The clatter, the clamor.

Who could sleep through all this?

The dropping of hammers. The loosing of tools.

The Stoning of the Devil

A little knowledge is a dangerous thing—why?

Because you do not know how little you know?

But then how can you know when you know enough

to know more than a little, to have many pieces

of knowledge that in aggregate mean understanding,

so that you are no longer in danger or a danger to others

or a danger but differently. I thought I knew about an awful thing

that had happened during the hajj, that many people had died

in a crush of human bodies, but then I heard years later

than an awful thing had happened during the hajj,

that many people had died in a crush of human bodies,

and I knew I didn't know whether it was the awful thing

I had remembered or another new and awful thing

that was also, awfully, the same thing. I now know that in 1994

270 pilgrims died and in 1998 118 pilgrims died

and in 2001 35 pilgrims died and in 2003

14 pilgrims died and in 2004 251 pilgrims died

and in 2006 346 pilgrims died and in 2015 2,411 pilgrims died and I don't know which of these I knew about first,

which means I don't know anything about any of them.

I know one way to think about a crush of bodies is to blame

the people whose bodies these are, to think that everyone

acting selfishly inevitably results in people trampled

into bodies, but I also know that thought is cruel and wrong.

It is more accurate to note that at six persons

per square meter individual action becomes impossible

and people behave not volitionally but like water,

carrying shock waves, filling crevasses, seeking everywhere

to distribute equally the fluid weight of persons.

But this is also cruel and wrong, to explain what happens to persons

by admitting that enough persons deny the very possibility

of thinking of what happens to them as something persons did.

Most of these pilgrims have died during a ritual named

the ramī al-jamarāt, or the Stoning of the Devil, which begins

on Eid al-Adha and refers to the hajj of Ibrāhīm, wherein

three temptations occurred: representing that of Ibrāhīm to spare

the life of Ismāīl, of Hājar to beseech him to spare Ismāīl, of Ismāīl to plead for his own life. At each of these Jibrayil tells Ibrāhīm

to pelt the devil with stones, and so each pilgrim must

do the same, striking one wall with seven pebbles, then on

the days following, each of the three walls with seven pebbles,

proceeding east to west. None of this knowledge is knowledge.

But each of those pilgrims is a person, unlike the drops that comprise

the fluid, the pebbles that comprise the mountain that collapses

to pebbles. What the devil wants of Ibrāhīm is for him to be selfish,

and that is what the angel exhorts Ibrāhīm to rebuke,

and what the pilgrims reject:

to think of others only in terms of the self. What the devil wants

is for us to look at the many and see none, to think of the many

but know no one.

Undercity

Unbearable above and unbearable alone: go below
to go within, make cavernous, dig and begin again.

The central alley of the undercity is where weddings occur,
where murders occur, where knife fights for the right

to lead the dwellers of the undercity occur, where the groom
lolls against the marital divan and the bride clutches

a bouquet of flowers grown in the artificial gardens
of the undercity by an old woman whose new name

suits her gifts, as does the name of every resident
of the undercity, or all those who found their way underground,

too ugly or too unloved or loved just enough to abandon,
who take their names from stories in books of old places,

beautiful places whose residents respected their monsters,
built palaces and mazes and castles for them, fed them

the best and the freshest and the bravest and the boldest,
built their whole civilizations around what gods compelled

them to acknowledge, around what they bred by breeding
with the residents of the mortal world, by bringing them

greater beauty and greater cruelty than a man can imagine.
All gods are built on whatever ruin remains of prior gods.

The cave is never closed, the season only changes.
The world is heaven's undercity, the undercity makes

of the world above a heaven. The ugly, the dispossessed.
The stealers of children, the bearer of chains. Below,

where for each figure of the above lives a flawed analogue.
Here, too, a Magdalene, a Lazarus, a Nazarene. Yes.

Madness to Believe

that things happen

without being made to happen—

madness to believe there is no maker

the ocean's agony and upset

is a giant risen from black marble

veined with white

like the tight but easily torn stitchery of waves

slipping against the giant

the jet of his fist

driven into the earth

the earth under the ocean is still the earth

cratered

and therefore creased

slow ocean

gelid black

viscous with cold

it only looks slow because it is enormous

      and far away

but seems to quicken as it approaches

      even though it slows

all you want from yourself

      and from whomever you made a child with

          is that as the wave advances

you will be strong enough

      to fling that child to them—

that they will be strong enough

          to catch that child

all you know

      as the wave advances

is that even if it is only for moments more

      you run

This Is Going to Hurt

No one who wants to see the world end wants to see it
from within the world's ending. They end *once upon a time,*
but then they want to close the book in which they are bound.

That sounds like something people would want, but you
would have to know them to say, and even then speak
as if you weren't one of them—just as I'm doing now.

Once, every living person needed, to a greater or lesser degree,
every other person. Now, every living person comes at the expense,
to a greater or lesser degree, of every other living person.

If you do not engage you afflict those who depend on your engagement,
and if you engage you afflict those who bear the cost
of your engagement. Do not worry, says the king, or if you wish

to put action to your worry, shop! And everyone laughs bitterly.
It's a stupid example and common, but its stupidity and obviousness
are what mark it as stupidly, obviously, commonly true.

Faced with an intractable problem or an insoluble dilemma,
everyone asks *Well, what can I do,* not to know the answer
but to avoid the implication of the question. What you can do

is a problem all by itself, all the things I am doing by being,
the cascade of consequences of what I choose and refuse,
what I want you to do compressed to what I want you to want.

Every single item we declare ourselves wise by refusing
to buy drives someone deeper into debt, denies someone else
the dim profit gleaned by the manufacture of an object we wish

did not exist or the provision of a service we wish no one desired.
You cannot have your wish for nothing granted without crippling
whoever needs you to take what they have to give without wishing

them away as well. It isn't that we believe anyone is innocent
of civilization; it is a question of how to behave once you know
everything you do or fail to do can only magnify your guilt.

I say *you* and *them* but I mean *me* and *mine,* joining to you
that to which you may not wish to be enjoined, and so
proving a fact by manufacturing one. That's civilization.

Some moderate their response to the alleged hysteria of cries
that the world is coming to its end by saying that no, it isn't
the world that is ending, it is civilization, but that is also false;

civilization will not end until people do, and even that misses
the point, which is that we are afraid what we find good about ourselves
will dwindle while what we find appalling will magnify,

and given that fear, the fact that a decline can take a very long time
means time is not something to treasure but rather something to dread,
a wickedness stretched over enough years to create greater wickedness,

a long enough spell for the people to make even more people,
every last one of whom will have the same claim on life, chief
of which is the production of more life, more living, more.

This happens to populations all the time, but that is no comfort
unless you are fine with thinking of yourself as a number of a number
and even if you are, others might not be. Humans are different, and not.

Humans are animals that have not yet decided whether
they are predators or prey, and, undecided, have become the worst
of both, herd and ravager, a murderer that thinks only of the threat

posed to it and never of the threat it poses. Some wish
for a superior animal to tell us we are not predator, not prey,
we are in aggregate everything we ever dreamed of being,

we are altogether like a god. What it means to be like a god
but not a god is what the category of magic is for: divine power
without divine judgment. But all stories of magic are tragedies.

Let's pretend every woman, child, and man on this planet receives
from this imaginary superior animal—this divinity—an elixir,
a potion, twenty jugs of which are a day of labor a thousand times

over, each person receiving twenty thousand jugs a day:
imagine the world, the wonder of it, the world enabled by magic,
the great asymmetrical castle of it, from few a radical exponent,

from a thin stem an impossible flowering. So much weight
sitting atop so little, so much breadth spun from so narrow a base.
No matter how unwieldy, any shape can be spun like a top,

can stand, but to stand it must spin or be spun forever.
To spin is to be in motion, and motion is labor, and to spin
is to work and make and make meaning of work.

Consider the lilies, how they grow; they toil not, they spin not,
and yet I say unto you that Solomon in all his glory was not so arrayed.
Solomon the king, Solomon the wise, Solomon the rich.

Every story of a people who have a story has a Solomon,
whether he or she is a mortal or an animal or a god.
When this Solomon asks God for wisdom he cites as his need

"the people," whom he calls great, that they cannot be numbered
nor counted for their multitude, for who could judge so many?
Not that the people were great in virtue and not in wisdom

for were they the former they would do good because it was good
and if the latter they would know themselves how to distinguish
the evil from the good, which is what it means to be wise.

The most famous proof of Solomon's wisdom is his solution
of a dispute between two women, each of whom insisted
she was the mother of the same baby, an argument Solomon

solves by offering to cut the child in half and apportion the remains
to each, at which prospect the real mother, horrified, recoils
and withdraws her claim, whereupon Solomon recognizes her

as the true mother and awards her the infant whole and intact.
The Bible is unclear about whether Solomon's wisdom resolves
in knowing how to identify the child's mother or in his original

solution to an insane problem: one more child in the people
who cannot be counted or numbered. Solomon the king:
700 wives, 300 concubines, of Egypt, of Moab, of Ammon

and Sidon and Hattusa. Everything in the known world when
the known world was not yet the whole world. Every living
creature danced at Solomon's command, save one animal

and when questioned that animal said it was only seeking
some unknown place, and having found that place and found
it rich in gold and wonders, Solomon wanted that place too.

This is the king to whom God gave wisdom, this is what
the wise do. There is no animal in the world to take the place
of God but even if there were, God is not so wise as to see

what the wise do with the gift of wisdom. Human animals
altogether: these will be the god of their individual members.
Every single animal if faced with a great enough threat will revert

to some random, desperate action: a twisting, a spasming,
a madness. With all the ways to make an animal insane
one would think that madness is why animals were made.

An animal, starving, who is unable to find food, will simply
continue looking until it no longer can and starves and dies.
But an animal who can see food it cannot reach will go mad.

An animal given more food than it can eat might eat itself
to death. Do you think of yourself in terms of what you are good
at or what you are good for? Live long enough and someone

may ask of you terrible things, and you may promise them that if
they grow ill or deranged they can trust that you will help them die.
You do not know if you choose to believe this is because they find you

full of mercy or lacking mercy entirely. Someone has to sit
with the body and so you sit with the body. Someone has to dispose
of the body and so you dispose of the body. Some are always surprised

by horror or disaster or numbers. Some rehearse the death
of everyone they know because the world performs for them
those deaths time and time over, and it is not fair or just and still

it keeps happening, mostly to those to whom it has already happened.
There is only so much preparation one can do: you can manage some pain
but there is always a pain that deranges the mind, and it doesn't matter

if you get to that pain by increment of amount or by unique kind,
for even if you know and remember the derangement
you can never tolerate it or master it or grow immune to pain.

You are brave until you are not. You endure until you cannot.
Some believe that the only relationship to pain is endurance
but these people have not yet known deranging pain,

because they do not know that a self capable
of endurance is an allowance of relief from pain, that pain
burns away the self that endures as if the self were a raindrop

in a fire, which at first may appear whole if variable, whole
if fragile, but will sooner or later be torn in half, its parts
rent apart, until nothing that is not fire can be in fire.

You don't know which injustice will consume you.
When Solomon raises the baby by its feet before the women
and says, *This is going to hurt,* one woman imagines a pain

she can endure and one woman imagines a pain she imagines
she cannot, but neither knows, and neither is the pain
of the baby cut in half. This is going to hurt. Even the exceptional

is common. The mortal know they are not immortal
and the impoverished know that increase is not forthcoming.
Grand tragedies do not erase quotidian ones. You have had them

and you have made them with no one to remedy or adjudicate.
After my father died I slept in the apartment we had been forced to vacate
and all night I thought about how to imagine one of many.

In the morning I locked the door, slipped the key through the slot
and I thought *This is bad* but also *This is nothing.* Most have it worse.
But bad is a degree of worse. I thought *This can get worse* and it did.

But what would have been better for us that did not worsen others?
The only good view of the failure of civilization, one
that either could never have been kind and thus failed

from its very conception or could have been kind and was not
and thus failed in its own execution, is the imagination of pain,
an apocalypse one can watch but not live, a rehearsal

that can never be the show. Everything is always falling, so
fall as slowly as you can. The dead are always from the future,
they are always sending reports of what can go wrong and will.

I am facing a man threatening to cleave a baby, I am holding a baby
no one will claim, I am reporting from the edge of the end
of the world I know, here's what I see, do what you can.

We shouldn't always do what we can. But sometimes we should.
I say this is going to hurt because this is going to hurt.
When my parents said it to me I thought they thought

it would make things hurt less, but it was just to remind me
that the value of my imagination was how limited it could be.
We imagined the wreck we've made and still we made it,

but maybe the wreck itself was the wrong thing to imagine.
Make less pain by imagining more pain, the pain that isn't your own.
When we leave this place it will be empty of persons.

No one will miss us. No one would. Still: do what you can.
You can imagine an empty room but cannot live in one.
You can imagine an empty world but cannot live in one.

But while it persists you can only persist with it.
Do what you can to solve a problem that cannot be solved,
until there is no one left to miss what never should have been.

Where Else

A shelter.

A clipper ship, a frigate, sailing on an orbit around the sun,
    sure as an orrery on a copper wire.

A cabinet.

On the other side of inward-opening doors: cabins, a cloister.

On the spinning drum of a ship, between worlds.

A bowl carved out of a mountain.

A pocked caldera.

A hole bored into a cliff above a crescent-shaped bay.

In rushes, in reeds.

In gardens, in cemeteries, in glades.

On the layer below the layer of great tectonic upheaval,
    above the layer of lucid oceans.

The office behind the office behind the door with the closed blinds.

The folly, the gazebo, the hammock.

An estate, a quarters on the estate, the flat perfect grass of the estate.

An escarpment, a crevasse in the desert.

A reef, a sandbar, a skiff half submerged.

An enormous brass egg, a treasure room, a storehouse.

A blanket hung between branches.

A palace, a prison.

A shell, a shadow, a nautilus. A darkness.

A not here. A never here.

Tableau Vivant

I wanted to know the scene

not by knowing it

but by seeing it.

To know that you were there

does not place you there,

does not allow you

to recollect who was where,

who wore what,

to even recall who or what.

I wanted it back not to be back,

but to have again

all that information,

so thick I couldn't tell

I was ignorant with it.

But how to ask.

She placed a hand to her head

and closed her eyes

and said, *Now let me see.*

Not like an old woman,

but like an old idea of an old woman.

Let me see.

How can I make out of these bodies

a machine to do what I cannot

when each body in the machine

suffers the same ignorance I do?

We are all of us alive now,

but each of us who once was

is wholly dead—

no more the thing we were

than the thing we will become.

I can see him as clearly I can see you

standing right here before me

this very instant.

Help me move the bodies into place,

where I know they must go

because I know where they have been.

Paint me a picture whereby

I do not know what

any of this looks like any longer.

I move into the setting.

And the bodies, too, move.

Spirit Measure

Please take this as a token of my affection. Or, think hard about this
object, even though I've made its meaning plain. When the widow hands
the watch to the spiritualist's assistant, she wants to know that the object
is, in fact, thinking about her. How cavalier the dead are, to have left
so many items without impressing upon the living the importance of
each. The face impresses itself upon the shroud, but when the dead man
beneath it spoke he said, *noli me tangere* (touch me not). If you knew the
provenance of an object just by touching it you would touch nothing, for
anything you touched would declare the means of its making and how
it found its way to you, and that would be terrible, like life in death, like
life in things we need to be dead so that we can use them for living. The
medium translates, but that is like using a handkerchief to grasp some-
thing sacred or vile: you still have to touch the handkerchief, you have to
touch gloves to wear gloves. A medium makes for a bad translator. What
does this object say to you? Touch me not, which means *unhand me,*
which means *let go.*

Zato-no-Ichi

In *New Tale of Zatoichi* the blind swordsman—

played by the sublime Shintaro Katsu

who at its filming cannot know that he will always be Zatoichi—

is being hunted by Yasuhiko, the brother of a man he has killed

but Zatoichi wants no more killing.

So behind Zatoichi's delight in life—

which we measure by his gambling

though his gambling is proof of his low station

and discern in his sensuality and his masseur's hands

though this work too proves that of all

Zatoichi is the lowest and the least—

behind this capacity for joy is killing

and behind that killing another reservoir of joy

in killing which Zatoichi fears is his true calling

fearing also that his response to that call

is the act of orienting himself by his own voice

for it is of rage and powerlessness and resentment

at being blind without station subordinate to lesser men

and as such lessened himself that Zatoichi attended so well

to his swordmaster Banno and thus dug the pit

out of which he is forever crawling.

* * *

In *New Tale of Zatoichi* the swordmaster Banno speaks well

of his former pupil the man whose skill he admires

even as he beholds in him a drunkard a wanderer a gangster

who in abdicating his great gift for murder loses

the only coin that cannot be stolen from him but in murdering

loses even the hope of a respectability that he cannot achieve.

* * *

Yayoi the sister of Banno remembers the Zatoichi

that Zatoichi cannot allow himself to remember

who even as he strove to master that which would undo him

was a righter of wrongs

a decent man who knows enough of his own indecency

to be ashamed and appalled to be a drunkard and a gangster

apologetic for being a drunkard and a gangster

Yayoi sees in him what blind Zatoichi cannot see:

that his knowledge of his incapacity for virtue proves his virtue.

* * *

This is the paradox of the blind swordsman Zatoichi

who must know his position in the world

because he cannot see himself at home in it

unlike Banno who though accomplished and proud

is wicked and greedy

and would sell his own sister to warlords and unrepentant killers

both Banno and Yasuhiko unable to admit that their flaws are wounds

they insist on carving into themselves and from which issue fonts of blood

by which the innocent are swept away.

* * *

As we watch we can see on the face of Yayoi her refusal of her brother Banno

and the suitor her brother has found for her

but we cannot see for her a way out

a way she sees in Zatoichi the drunkard the gangster

who when she asks him if he will marry her and leave this place

and go elsewhere though all of Edo is at this time corrupt and unkind responds with a look or a sequence of looks

that depict clearly a blind man looking forward

into a future he has not allowed himself to imagine

for imagining it would force him to admit

the Zatoichi behind Zatoichi

that hope before the rage.

* * *

And that after rage the remorse

that now disallows his looking forward

and his sublime face is many faces

and all the ways one can be afraid

for Zatoichi the blind swordsman knows

that a life of indignity and squalor is nothing

compared to the humiliation of revealing his hope

that he could be seen or known as good or as desiring to be good

and watching we know that the number of faces a blind man must make

to remain unseen by those who cannot see

is agony

is a number without end.

* * *

When the blind swordsman pledges out loud to renounce

the ways Yayoi knows him

even though Yayoi needs no such pledge nor asks for one

we know and she knows that Zatoichi is doomed

and that she is doomed thereby.

* * *

For Yayoi seeing her brother as without worth

and Zatoichi of great worth needs nothing

but to go away from this Edo to another Edo

to neither of which she owes anything

but Zatoichi being blind to this must ask of his teacher Banno

a man in every way less than he

permission and forgiveness and having asked

receives the contempt and disgust that he has allowed himself to believe

he deserves.

* * *

In this forbearance even Yasuhiko the brother of the murdered man

whose murder sets in motion the whole tale

the ending of which we now know and cannot help but know

even Yasuhiko sees that Zatoichi is honorable and decent

and would rather quit his claim on his life

as Zatoichi himself would relinquish that life

rather than disappoint Yayoi whom he knows he will but cannot disappoint

this leaves only Banno

who because he cannot know what he is

but can only believe that he is something other than what he is

destroys everything

his blindness to his own pettiness and lust for dominion forcing Zatoichi

to do that which he has sworn not to do.

* * *

"I have cut those I should not have cut, killed those I should not have killed"

Having seen the one good man she knows prove to himself

that he can never be the man she knows him to be

Yayoi pauses and in pausing sets the tableau at whose center rests Zatoichi

who has returned to the posture he took before killing

the posture like the killing indistinguishable from what it punctuates

Yayoi the heartbroken flees into an Edo unknown

and Zatoichi the blind swordsman who cannot see her go

knows she is going and cannot, cannot allow himself to know that she goes

not because of what he is but because of what he will not believe he is.

* * *

In *New Tale of Zatoichi* the sublime Shintaro Katsu

depicts Zatoichi the blind swordsman

drunkard beggar lowest and least

stands in a tableau he makes but cannot see

cannot see who is he and who he cannot believe he is

Zatoichi, the blind man, the man who cannot see.

"Is There in Truth No Beauty?"

Don't get excited; it's an episode of *Star Trek*.

People recall them via the formula whereby

x happens to Spock or Spock does x,

so it's the one where Spock goes blind from looking directly into

a box so alien that humans go mad at the mere sight of it—

so that happens, too, he goes blind and he goes mad.

He's helped from the latter condition by someone who shares the former,

Dr. Miranda Jones, who is fascinating and never appears again.

She is a little bit telepathic and a lot blind, but disguises that last fact

with the best and most useful dress in the galaxy,

beaded and jeweled, a machine that is also a garment,

a veil that reads the world.

You can tell from the skin of it that it glitters—

from fingers across the texture the illumination whispers itself.

Flawed pearl, which is pearl, and steel, which is sheets of steel, folded.

Diamond, the making of pearl inverted.

God, I prayed, *give it to me, so that I may never be caught unawares again.*

Over skin or in sheathes or affixed to surfaces,

lacquered and layered, bound

& likewise a lie of the uniform, the absolute.

The discerning costume jewelry, like a bejeweled box of jewels,

like a book barnacled with trinkets.

Pearls placed on my wrists would be receivers

with which I could hear rivers and bays,

and from stellar steel I could acquire signals

floated on magnetic waves,

diamonds that would transmit harmonies

from the hottest, heaviest weather of the moving mantle

of alternate earths, each one fantastic.

Like the good doctor, I wanted to be equipped not for one plane

but for planets, immersed, detecting and undetectable,

delectable, beset by data,

with a net flung over the box of the skull,

its every point a jewel or a miniature and perfectly tooled device.

And equidistant from each point the music or mind,

held together with clasps or clefts or thoughts

that when opened and scattered

go from precious to semiprecious to base.

Please God let me slip into something more comfortable.

Though it would be lovely, too, just to be lovely

and at the end of the day cast off all information,

like the doctor, intuit no more than what others offer,

in darkness, naked, unknowing save for what

the world would have to touch me to tell.

Structural Color

The broken blue eyes do not work well

but offer excellent optical illusions,

like the feathers of the jay and the peacock,

like the motion of mother of pearl

or the flash of butterfly wings,

the industrial sheen of beetle shells

and the oil slicks they resemble,

like the iridescent surface of bubbles

floating in the optical illusion of the sky,

which is not blue, but only looks that way.

Hothouse

A rose, rose. A violet, violet. A jade, jade.
No. The architecture of each, a refusal.

Rose is not rose nor violet violet nor jade jade.
But each is what it is, not what it seems.

What each seems is what of each gets seen.
Though what we see isn't the thing seen.

The petals of the rose are violet and jade.
Thus the petals of the rose look, to us, rose.

The shape of the violet absorbs all but violet.
The violet we see is the violet a violet rejects.

A rose is a rose is a rose, but not as a rose.
Jade is the name of jade, not the jade named.

The Concealed

To express an essence of the dead to the living
takes storytelling, and the story I like best to tell is this:
that once when my sister and I were meowing

at our cat, who obligingly meowed back,
our father turned quickly upon us and said
Don't do that, and struck by his vehemence

we stopped but also could not help but ask him
Why not, and he answered, *Because you don't know
what you are saying,* and this was so true

that we were struck dumb, which is both what we were
and what he wanted us to be. To say you don't know
what you are saying makes sense but it does not

make sense to say do not look, you do not know
what you are looking at, because it is unclear
that looking is something you do in the way

that saying is something you do though clearly
you can be mistaken in both, you can say the wrong
thing, you can see incorrectly. Galen describes the eye

as a series of tunicae—garments—and like garments
they are not all of the same weight or color or substance.
When you say you like what someone is wearing

you don't say "I like how your jacket occludes your blouse,
I like how your scarf almost but not entirely obscures
your skin." You don't know what you are saying because

you don't know what you are looking at, because the thing
with which you are looking is not one thing but several,
as are the things at which you look. If you disrobe the eye

the eye disappears before its parts do, though as it goes
it goes strangely, for if you peel from the eye its lens
the eye that remains sees into ultraviolet, and thus

by removal sees what was always there. You don't know
what you are seeing. There are only so many tunics
to discard. A cat can see into the ultraviolet, which is why

its attention seems focused on what is not apparent.
Not every garment is like every other garment.
In the complex arrangement of family relationships

relayed by Matthew the Apostle, what precedes
the execution of John the Baptist is either his ability
or inability to accurately perceive the nature

of the relationships before him: it is the daughter
of Herod and Herodias who dances
for her father at the behest of her mother

who desires vengeance on John the Baptist, and so bidden
dances so well or so powerfully or so compellingly
that her father Herod, the king, grants her whatever

she wishes (that is whatever her mother, his wife, wishes)
and thus the beheading of the Baptist. Her name is Salome.
You don't know what you are saying: the name of Salome

is spoken neither by Matthew nor Mark but rather
by Flavius Josephus in his *Judean Antiquities,*
a term that surely includes the Bible but is not

equivalent to it. A feature of the Gospels that strikes
as strange only those who have bothered to read
them is that they tell different versions of the same

stories, each version adding or removing a layer
of detail, so that what constitutes the Bible is in fact
the relationship of many parts to a whole although

that whole in sum includes apocrypha and histories
like those of Flavius Josephus. When you say
Salome, it is equally true and false that you refer

to the biblical character, though everyone will know
what you mean even if you don't know quite
what you are saying. Salome, yes, Salome

who danced the dance of the seven veils,
the erotic implication of which is that whomever
gazes upon Salome sees Salome as veiled

but also obscured, so that the fewer garments
she wears the more clearly she can be seen
but also that not seeing her unveiled becomes

the entire point of gazing upon her. Salome,
the girl from the Bible, who danced the dance
of the seven veils, whose veils are not in the Bible

and who is herself only in the Bible
if you do not look and if you look, disappears
and reappears depending on what you are looking with.

When we say you do not know what you are saying
we are seeing that you do not know what you see,
that how you see and what you see are severed,

a head from a body, a sound from a sense,
a careful arrangement of surfaces, shifting,
just because seen are not the same as same.

& Juliet

Sclera, the collagen of the eye, thickens with time. It is the ciliary muscle that must move the lens but the lens, if given enough time, would harden into a geode, a rock iris, too dense for any muscle to move. And if it ceased to move, the eye would cease to see, for it evolved to detect motion, or difference, one form of which is the relationship between darkness and light. Eyes are born in the dark but not all of the dark. They are born in dusk, in dimness. The collagens of the cornea are arranged with such perfect geometrical regularity that it admits light, but the retina is what sees. The retina is brain. Wanting to be close, we built a blackout room as an experiment during that summer an eclipse threw crescent shadows on the ground and reminded us we had no idea how our eyes worked because we depended on them to do so much work for us. Two bodies in a black room, dependent on proprioception, erase all concept of distance, since distance depends on shadow, perspective on occlusion. Some forms of sight are only mapping, so that whatever moves, disappears; in other forms, anything stable projected on the retina vanishes. It was a dark room, the room that contained our bodies, but not perfectly black. The closest to perfect black is a substance of vertically aligned carbon nanotubes that absorb 99.965% of visible radiation. The sight of it confuses the mind, but light can be deferred in many ways. Some fall into fevers, and when they awake are blind.

Sidewinder

Down there. Something gleams,
a snake in grass, a stream in granite,
the murmur of motion conversant
with less motion, of animals and water
with trees and grass. It all moves
whether we note it or not,
the markers of what we made
identical to whatever we made them out of,
the interruption of the place
now the place itself. Above:
noise and life, glasses ringing
before they are shards, bolts
fixing that which, once fallen,
will leave the bolts that bound
the beams to rust in the grass.
I am never sad. I don't wish to miss this,
which means that I am glad
I saw it but will not regret
that it is gone. I want nothing,
not even to be free of desire.

Kwaidan

But sometimes the dead are awful,
their demands.

This is the lesson of Hoichi
the Earless.

The painted set is somehow larger
than the world.

The seas give way to paintings
of the sea.

Stories of death on the sea
become songs.

Hoichi the blind biwa player
performs them.

It is not above the dead
to trick the blind.

The dead are imperious
and compel servant ghosts.

Ghosts are imperious
and compel Hoichi.

He yields to the dead,
their vanity.

He cannot see the sutra
on his skin.

His ears, forgotten,
are forsaken.

Nothing has ever looked
so beautiful.

Nothing has ever sounded
so beautiful.

Because of the dead
Hoichi cannot see.

Playing to the dead
Hoichi cannot hear.

Claire Lenoir

What happens in the short story "Claire Lenoir"

is strange.

Later adapted by its author, Villiers de L'Isle-Adam,

into the novel *Tribulat Bonhomet,* the tale

features the eponymous positivist who

elects to visit his old friend Césaire Lenoir

and his wife Claire.

During the voyage (for in decadent fiction

the plot often advances at the pace of transport

characteristic of the era of decadent fiction)

the positivist befriends a young lieutenant

who discloses (with the alacrity of revelation

characteristic of decadent fiction) that he,

the lieutenant, has recently pursued a romance

with a married woman whose description

matches that of the wife of the positivist's friend,

Claire Lenoir.

After this interlude the lieutenant ventures

to his next post, somewhere in the South Seas,

while the positivist proceeds to the estate

of the Lenoirs.

Before he arrives at their home he pauses

to rest in a café and reads in a discarded paper

an article that tells of how no less an authority

than the L'Académie des Sciences du Paris

has verified that in the eyes of animals

butchered for our nourishment remains the image

of the butcher's stroke, that the last thing

a mind sees before its extinction is the image

of whatever effected that extinction. *Via camera.*

What then follows at the Lenoir estate

is also strange:

a lengthy conversation between positivist,

friend, and friend's wife about death, the real,

the soul, the beyond. Without warning

Césaire Lenoir falls ill, but before he dies

he learns of his wife's infidelity and swears

vengeance upon her lover, even if he must

visit from the afterlife.

One year later, Claire Lenoir herself

is on the verge of death, hounded there

by guilt and recurrent dreams of Césaire,

dressed in blood on the shores of an unknown

island. The positivist is shocked,

for only days before did he learn of the fate

of his acquaintance the lieutenant, beheaded

by cannibals in Polynesia, for the opposite of the positivist

is perforce "the savage" and "the unknown."

At this, Claire expires, and discerning in her eyes

an indistinct image the positivist employs

his ophthalmoscope and clarifies the vision,

which he is horrified to discover is of a man

who resembles Césaire holding the severed head

of a man who resembles the deceased lieutenant.

To understand the crisis this induces

in the positivist is to appreciate how his acceptance

of the natural fact of a photographic film

of the cause of death peeled from the lenses

of the dead means he must therefore accept

that the immediate cause of Claire's death

is simply the sight of what she could not have seen,

an event that itself seems to have been caused

solely by the will of the dying Césaire.

The strangeness of positivism is strange:

it allows hatred and incomprehension

even as it implores us to believe what we see and only

what we can deduce therefrom but suggests

that what occurs in the mind is imposed there

by experience. Is it the horror of the decadent fiction

that we can deduce a mind from the operation

of a camera but cannot bear the thought of a mind

that is not the camera that feeds it. Knowledge

would destroy the positivist. Knowledge

destroys anyone whose knowledge is that they knew it

when they saw it, that they knew to know is to see.

Mosaic Style

For the mosaic portrait, your directions are these:
first near, then far.

If near is azure glass or white plaster,
you are doing well

and if far is the face of one of the great and good,
you are doing well.

If near is the face of those who go unpainted,
a sheaf of cracks

in the face of the glaze, a blue maiden broken
in a blue mood,

and far is nothing but blue, its affect and aura,
a dim bloom

swollen so that the white veins no longer course
across the face

of the great and good, if the face is now diffused
to blue paint

even though you know that paint is a portrait,
all edges,

not a liquid into which you could step
but a wall

that would resist your entrance and even
cut you

for your efforts. Near, no one can see what you see
as you see it,

and far, no one can know why you do not see
what they see.

Step back. Farther, farther, until even blue blurs out,
no paint

to paint faces with, no glass to find faces in,
farther, by far.

Castrovalva

the hill and stones of the mountain
close grained and dust colored by moonlight
that whitens the silver planes of the clouds
that float and recur over Castrovalva
its gardens and squares gray going to green with the sun
that rises and sets against the four-cornered walls
goldenrod tides rising and falling
against the walls and towers like the rain
from the lake
within & without
above & below
a window without glass
a window that mirrors

a city still if and as everyone in it knows every other
we know every resident of the city-village of castle-valve
every washerwoman also a tinsmith
every tool of at least two purposes
to be inside the walls of Castrovalva is to be atrial & sororal
on either side of the courtyard's doors is the courtyard
Castrovalva curves Castrovalva cures
Castrovalva has no queen Castrovalva has no king
every book in the library of Castrovalva binds the same words
every tapestry hung on the walls of Castrovalva depicts you
in a stone chamber watching the tapestry's tale
single thread behind & through above the warp & below

you cannot exit Castrovalva by means of entrances
beneath the city of Castrovalva lies the castle-valve
tunnels and sinks
one's city is one's home
the home of one's home is also one's home
the valve of the castle opens upon the castle

and so fall the twins of Castrovalva
to be outside the walls of Castrovalva is to fall forever
down the side of the mountain
irregular roads
steps sidereal
for the lake as you approach becomes the sky above
and you descend again into the city from which you fell

Castrovalva turns Castrovalva returns
the city the puzzled gear of its own rotation

as are the sky and the lake
between which hangs the castle-valve
so on its walls and in its chambers hang
the polished mirror-metals of Castrovalva
you cannot see without
without seeing within

above as below
doubled
sororal

you see yourself seeing
one sister sees in her sister a seeing
and says as they fall *welcome*
if this city is not my city
if my sister is not my sister
if her city is not my city
where then shall I go to make a home

The Social Realism of Negative Space

To focus only on this is childish,
and God and the world need you
to put away childish things.

There were people, they paid
or did not pay taxes, wars transpired,
plastics accumulated massively,

the shore acquired shit and algae,
the window wouldn't close and
the mirror got sticky with condensate,

the real sky and not the notional sky
slowly filled with debris of martial
and commercial origin and broadcast

many very special episodes now in syndication
watched by many people in jail
and those the luckiest of the jailed

but some are in solitary and none
deserve that and most shouldn't be
anywhere but home though home

too is often hellish and you cannot
see celestial bodies from inside
catacombs and cells or even

within toxic houses even when
they have holes in the roof just
like you cannot check pretty

books out of the library if you
don't know where it is or
if it even is and even if it was

you don't have time because
you are trying hard not to die.
None of this happened in a dream.

It happened in the murder capital
of Florida. But you can see that
the murder capital of Florida

is epic with these dreams
and dreams like these because
they are how we endured

the state of being awake, the art
that was not for art's sake, for
fuck's sake, but for the sake

of somewhere to go to survive
being here, of junk for the sake
of junk because that was the yard

you had and you worked
with the world you had
but sometimes: wonder.

That which is perfect has not come.
That which is in part continues.
You think this mirrored, dim,

but look at the shape between
the face and the face it faces,
know also as I am known.

False Topographical Map of the Land of Grasses and Flowers

Again, just turn upside down:

the garden is water now, vapor and azure,

blue duotint. The deckled edges are cumulus

and towering cumulus, and cirrus is the wash

of the marble from which the garden is made.

On occasion a spiral of activity will twist upward,

and on many more occasions the speed

of the shifting ground, cloud against cloud,

will snap in half and half again spindles of light.

Sometimes the world will fall apart,

a shuttle of unwoven rain. And sometimes

after that the false blue of the night sky,

absent stars you cannot distinguish,

absent everything but the perpetual moon.

Mise en abyme

Even without the figural

the figures exist: the image

disappears into itself

but only by being placed

before itself or within

itself by confusing

upon and *within*

themselves. My sister says

He is looking at me funny

and my mother says

He always looks like that.

It's true: I make the face

with my face. I only

know what I look

like when I look

at myself, but I look

mostly at what isn't there.

I know what is isn't

like this abyss but look,

the hole in the shield

is what makes the shield

whole.

Tricky

Our paper arts allow us
to render on the square, the mountain.
Of lamina, make the valley and the sink.
Night and day, black on one side, white the other.
That it is flexible enough to take a crease,
stiff enough to keep one. Bent into butterflies
for brides, folded into cranes to teach flight.

Siege

Whatever was left of what was once the hothouse:

six wide windows, not perfectly parallel to the shore,

angled eastward so that the rising sun crosses upward,

across the beams that separate the windows.

Thin hems, barely perceptible.

Six wide windows, two floors, the upper open

to the lower, a single spiral staircase connecting them.

Here I slept.

On my back, head tipped to watch the world through the window

that was the empty square where once the window was:

abundant sky and churning seam of sea.

Seen so, that seam looked like a fortress, its edge high on a cliff.

The cliff, lilac-white stone, dim in darkness, illumined enough to climb.

The face of the cliff was a pearlescent wall of clouds.

The city was the sea.

All possible because of the moon.

Had I seen the moon it would have been a hole in the wall of the cliff.

And I would think the sleeping city afloat on vertical leagues of silver.

Seen properly, none of it would ever have been.

To lay siege to the night's city, sleep upside down,

hung halfway between the walls of a box of glass.

Let me tell you why the moon

because once it was only yellow as dust

or an icy isolated white

only as round as its frayed edge

a shape of a surface

on which the oil of the eye

a shape crimped to oblivion with a blink

a scrim on which cast the lashes of the open eye

imaginary weight that wrought the crest

of all our never-ending floods

watcher of water I wanted to seep into every fissure

and shatter the castle

presence that was a hole in my pending dark

because it was only an idea I could not see

I prayed to God to let me see

I begged a god I could not see for sight

and then

rightly for the first time

the moon

Notes

Agfa Lupe 8x: The phosphor bars of the Sony Trinitron hypnotized many nearsighted children of my generation, and Grover is the muppet who attempted to teach us the difference between near and far.

Wait Until Dark: This poem refers to the 1967 film version directed by Terence Young based on the 1966 play by Frederick Knott.

Landlords: The curses here are derived mainly from the book of Leviticus. The E. L. Mustee Durastall is real.

The Interchangeable World of the Micronauts: The title refers to the promotional descriptor in the late 1970s and early 1980s of modular toys based on the popular Japanese toy line by Takara. Projectile hazard, choking hazard, good times.

Psychotic Mood Swing: Saint Anthony of Padua is the patron saint of lost souls, lost causes, and lost objects.

Viridescent: All the plants cited here are (or were) to be found in Florida.

Destiny and Mystique: The issue in question is *Uncanny X-Men* #142, published February 1981.

Vertumnal: The title and poem refer not only to the Roman god but also to the painting by the Mannerist Giuseppe Arcimboldo.

Space: This is a reconstruction of Filippo Brunelleschi's invention of perspective drawing techniques, and owes a debt to the analysis of those events by Arthur Zajonc in his *Catching the Light: The Entwined History of Light and Mind*, published 1995.

I will show you . . . : Castrovalva is a lithograph by M. C. Escher, and the quote is from a Dutch critic cited by Bruno Ernst in *The Magic Mirror of M.C. Escher.* "Castrovalva" is also the title of a 1982 episode of *Doctor Who.*

Castle-Valve and *Castrovalva* both draw on the epigraph to *Driftglass* by Samuel R. Delany.

Fortifications of the Land of Grasses and Flowers is a response to "Dawn" by Federico García Lorca, translated by Eliot Weinberger.

Pilgrims refers to an especially dispiriting episode from Matsuo Bashō's pilgrimages.

Mine: Phosphate mining is one of Florida's many egregious ecological errors. Every now and again one of these mines will collapse into a sinkhole and corrupt the aquifer. The area in which this is likely to occur is called Bone Valley, and the industry was precipitated by the arrival of the Florida Southern Railway in Arcadia, Florida, in 1886.

Tertullian: The text I am interrupting here is drawn from the *Apologeticum* and *De Testimonio animae.*

There is but one . . . : the title refers to a line from *Le Mythe de Sisyphe* by Albert Camus.

Five Million Years to Earth, produced in 1967 by Hammer Film Productions, was written by Nigel Kneale and directed by Roy Ward Baker.

Here Comes the Flood refers to the eponymous painting by Rob Gonsalves.

The Uncertain Value of Human Life: In cave diving, different levels of salinity can create the optical illusion that the more translucent top layer is, in fact, not liquid at all but air. Divers sometimes get confused and will remove their breathing equipment when still entirely under water.

Generation Mechanism: "Harbor wave" is the literal translation of the word "tsunami." I am especially indebted to *Facing the Wave* by Gretel Ehrlich, published 2013.

The Stoning of the Devil: The number of deaths for some of these incidents remains a matter of dispute between state officials and other organizations.

Tableau vivant can refer equally to living figures posed and photographed to resemble paintings and to paintings made by reliance on posed figures.

Spirit Measure: In John 20:17, Jesus is alleged to have responded to being recognized by Mary Magdalene by saying "touch me not" or, in Latin, *noli mi tangere.*

Zato-no-Ichi: The actor Shintaro Katsu starred in twenty-six Zatoichi feature films. *New Tale of Zatoichi* was the third of these, directed by Tozuko Tanaka in 1963.

"Is There in Truth No Beauty?": This is a 1968 episode of *Star Trek,* written by Jean Lisette Aroeste and directed by Ralph Senensky and featuring Diana Muldaur as Dr. Miranda.

The Concealed: The only Salome mentioned in the Bible is a disciple of Jesus; the better-known figure is described but never named. Many details we associate with her narrative are derived from subsequent commentaries and elaborations, such as the dance of the seven veils, which appears in the Strauss opera, but he got it from Wilde, and *he* got it from Flaubert. It's also worth noting that when Josephus mentions Salome, he says nothing about John the Baptist at all.

& Juliet: The substance referred to is Vantablack, and currently, the only artist licensed to use it is Anish Kapoor.

The tale of Hoichi the Earless is one of four narratives anthologized in *Kwaidan,* Masaki Kobayashi's 1965 horror film based on Lafcadio Hearn's translations of Japanese myths and folktales.

Claire Lenoir: Villiers de L'Isle-Adam is one of the great also-rans of speculative literature, a hot mess of romantic, symbolist, and Catholic impulses and practices. The assumption upon which Claire Lenoir depends, however, was not his invention, but was in wide circulation at the time. I am indebted to Simon Ings's description in *A Natural History of Seeing: The Art and Science of Vision,* published 2008.

The Social Realism of Negative Space draws upon 1 Corinthians.

Mise en abyme: Though the technique is now more often associated with painting and film (as well as in recursive stories or frame stories), its origin is in heraldry.

Let me tell you why . . . : Severe myopia turns every light source into a sphere that approximates the action of the eye itself, so that when you look at, say, the moon, you can see the shadows of your own eyelids around its perimeter.

Acknowledgments

Grateful acknowledgment to the readers and editors of the following journals for publishing these poems.

Academy of American Poets Poem-a-Day: "Hothouse"
American Poetry Review: "The Concealed"
Bennington Review: "Decimation" and "Wait Until Dark"
Black Warrior Review: "Look Up"
DIAGRAM: "& Juliet"
Ecotone: "Descender" and "Viridescent"
Michigan Quarterly Review: "Claire Lenoir" and "Pilgrims"
POETRY: "The Interchangeable World of the Micronauts"
Typo Magazine: "Fontanel"

Thanks to Erika Stevens and the wonderful people of Coffee House Press. Thanks to Hilary Lowe and Michael Gustafson and the staff of Literati Bookstore in Ann Arbor. Thank you Linda Gregerson, Maureen McLane, Paula Mendoza, Sarah Messer, Paisley Rekdal, and Keith Taylor.

This book is for my parents, with gratitude and love.

Coffee House Press began as a small letterpress operation in 1972 and has grown into an internationally renowned nonprofit publisher of literary fiction, essay, poetry, and other work that doesn't fit neatly into genre categories.

Coffee House is both a publisher and an arts organization. Through our *Books in Action* program and publications, we've become interdisciplinary collaborators and incubators for new work and audience experiences. Our vision for the future is one where a publisher is a catalyst and connector.

LITERATURE
is not the same thing as
PUBLISHING

Funder Acknowledgments

Coffee House Press is an internationally renowned independent book publisher and arts nonprofit based in Minneapolis, MN; through its literary publications and *Books in Action* program, Coffee House acts as a catalyst and connector— between authors and readers, ideas and resources, creativity and community, inspiration and action.

Coffee House Press books are made possible through the generous support of grants and donations from corporations, state and federal grant programs, family foundations, and the many individuals who believe in the transformational power of literature. This activity is made possible by the voters of Minnesota through a Minnesota State Arts Board Operating Support grant, thanks to the legislative appropriation from the arts and cultural heritage fund. Coffee House also receives major operating support from the Amazon Literary Partnership, the Jerome Foundation, The McKnight Foundation, Target Foundation, and the National Endowment for the Arts (NEA). To find out more about how NEA grants impact individuals and communities, visit www.arts.gov.

Coffee House Press receives additional support from the Elmer L. & Eleanor J. Andersen Foundation; the David & Mary Anderson Family Foundation; the Buuck Family Foundation; Fredrikson & Byron, P.A.; Dorsey & Whitney LLP; the Fringe Foundation; Kenneth Koch Literary Estate; the Knight Foundation; the Rehael Fund of the Minneapolis Foundation; the Matching Grant Program Fund of the Minneapolis Foundation; Mr. Pancks' Fund in memory of Graham Kimpton; the Schwab Charitable Fund; Schwegman, Lundberg & Woessner, P.A.; the U.S. Bank Foundation; VSA Minnesota for the Metropolitan Regional Arts Council; and the Woessner Freeman Family Foundation in honor of Allan Kornblum.

The Publisher's Circle of Coffee House Press

Publisher's Circle members make significant contributions to Coffee House Press's annual giving campaign. Understanding that a strong financial base is necessary for the press to meet the challenges and opportunities that arise each year, this group plays a crucial part in the success of Coffee House's mission.

Recent Publisher's Circle members include many anonymous donors, Suzanne Allen, Patricia A. Beithon, the E. Thomas Binger & Rebecca Rand Fund of the Minneapolis Foundation, Robert & Gail Buuck, Claire Casey, Louise Copeland, Jane Dalrymple-Hollo, Ruth Stricker Dayton, Jennifer Kwon Dobbs & Stefan Liess, Mary Ebert & Paul Stembler, Chris Fischbach & Katie Dublinski, Kaywin Feldman & Jim Lutz, Sally French, Jocelyn Hale & Glenn Miller, the Rehael Fund-Roger Hale/Nor Hall of the Minneapolis Foundation, Randy Hartten & Ron Lotz, Dylan Hicks & Nina Hale, William Hardacker, Jeffrey Hom, Carl & Heidi Horsch, Amy L. Hubbard & Geoffrey J. Kehoe Fund, Kenneth Kahn & Susan Dicker, Stephen & Isabel Keating, Kenneth Koch Literary Estate, Cinda Kornblum, Lenfestey Family Foundation, Sarah Lutman & Rob Rudolph, the Carol & Aaron Mack Charitable Fund of the Minneapolis Foundation, George & Olga Mack, Joshua Mack & Ron Warren, Gillian McCain, Mary & Malcolm McDermid, Sjur Midness & Briar Andresen, Maureen Millea Smith & Daniel Smith, Peter Nelson & Jennifer Swenson, Marc Porter & James Hennessy, Enrique Olivarez, Jr. & Jennifer Komar, Alan Polsky, Robin Preble, Jeffrey Sugerman & Sarah Schultz, Alexis Scott, Nan G. & Stephen C. Swid, Patricia Tilton, Stu Wilson & Melissa Barker, Warren D. Woessner & Iris C. Freeman, Margaret Wurtele, Joanne Von Blon, and Wayne P. Zink & Christopher Schout.

For more information about the Publisher's Circle and other ways to support Coffee House Press books, authors, and activities, please visit www.coffeehouse press.org/support or contact us at info@coffeehousepress.org.

Raymond McDaniel is the author of *Special Powers and Abilities, Saltwater Empire,* and *Murder (a violet),* a National Poetry Series selection.

The Cataracts was typeset by Bookmobile Design & Digital Publisher Services. Text is set in Warnock Pro.